THE WOMEN'S LAND ARMY

Neil R. Storey & Molly Housego

SHIRE PUBLICATIONS

Published by Shire Publications Ltd.
PO Box 883, Oxford, OX1 9PL, UK
PO Box 3985, New York, NY 10185-3985, USA
Email: shire@shirebooks.co.uk   www.shirebooks.co.uk

© 2012 Neil R. Storey and Molly Housego.

First published 2012.
Transferred to digital print on demand 2015.

A CIP catalogue record for this book is available from the
British Library.

Shire Library no. 694.   ISBN-13: 978 0 74781 163 3

Neil R. Storey and Molly Housego have asserted their
right under the Copyright, Designs and Patents Act, 1988,
to be identified as the authors of this book.

Designed by Tony Truscott Designs, Sussex, UK.
Typeset in Perpetua and Gill Sans.
Printed and bound in Great Britain.

COVER IMAGE
'We could do with thousands more like you' – A Women's
Land Army recruitment poster, c. 1944.

TITLE PAGE IMAGE
Cover of The Landswoman, December 1919.

CONTENTS PAGE IMAGE
Brooch presented as a token of gratitude by the Women's
Land Army.

MIX
Paper from
responsible sources
FSC   FSC® C013604
www.fsc.org

ACKNOWLEDGEMENTS
The authors would like to express their sincere thanks to
all those who have assisted and encouraged their research
into the WLA and WTC over the years, especially all those
wonderful women who have taken their time to share their
stories, memorabilia and friendship with us. We would
particularly like to record our thanks to: Sue Chippington
at the Imperial War Museum, Duxford; the National
Archives; Megan Dennis, Gressenhall Farm and
Workhouse Museum of Norfolk Life; the Norfolk
Federation of Women's Institutes; Robert Bell, Lilian
Ream Collection, Wisbech; Forestry Commission
Scotland; BBC Radio Norfolk; Helen Tovey and all the
team at Family Tree Magazine; Geoff Caulton; Ron and Jenny
Franklyn; John and Kitty Warnes; Paul and Kerry Nicholls;
Iris Tillett, Frieda Feetham, Dorothy Riches; Beryl Self,
Betty Smith, Grace Thurling and Daisy Robinson.
The photographs, badges and ephemera in this book
are from originals in the archives of the authors, unless
indicated otherwise.

IMAGE ACKNOWLEDGEMENTS
Ron Franklyn, page 18 (centre); Getty Images, pages 24
(lower), 40; Imperial War Museum, pages 8 (lower), 9, 12,
13 (both), 16, 17, 26 (lower), 31 (lower), 32 (upper and
lower), 33 (both), 35 (upper), 39 (lower), 42, 44 (lower),
45, 46; Lilian Ream Collection, page 39 (lower); Mary
Evans Picture Library, pages 24 (lower), 28.

All other images are from the author's collection.

IMPERIAL WAR MUSEUM COLLECTIONS
Many of the photos in this book come from the Imperial
War Museum's huge collections which cover all aspects of
conflict involving Britain and the Commonwealth since the
start of the twentieth century. These rich resources are
available online to search, browse and buy at
www.iwmcollections.org.uk. In addition to Collections
Online, you can visit the Visitor Rooms where you can
explore over 8 million photographs, thousands of hours of
moving images, the largest sound archive of its kind in the
world, thousands of diaries and letters written by people
in wartime and a huge reference library. To make an
appointment, call (020) 7416 5320, or e-mail
mail@iwm.org.uk. Website: www.iwm.org.uk

Shire Publications is supporting the Woodland Trust, the UK's leading woodland conservation charity, by funding the dedication of trees.

CONTENTS

NATIONAL SERVICE

WOMEN'S LAND ARMY

GOD SPEED THE PLOUGH
AND THE WOMAN WHO DRIVES IT"

SERIES W9.

H. G. GAWTHORN.

D.&6.&.LONDON

SOWING THE SEED

W OMEN have worked on Britain's farms in a variety of roles for as long
as there has been farming. In the centuries before the First World War
the roles of women in agriculture were predominantly in dairying (notably
butter making), poultry keeping, and at harvest time, when just about every
hand of the village from children to grandparents would be required in the
days before mechanisation. When war was declared in August 1914 thousands
of men from all walks of life, including thousands of farm workers,
patriotically rushed to join the colours but there was still a corn harvest to be
gathered in. Despite an estimated 100,000 agricultural workers leaving the
land to 'do their bit' in 1914, farmers did not see the depletion of workers on
the land as too much of a problem through the winter of 1914–15 but began
to feel the pinch in the spring and early summer of 1915, when it was noted
that farm work began to fall behind because of a lack of available labour.
Farmers were not keen on employing large numbers of women on the land,
however, and voiced concerns that they did not consider women physically
capable of tasks such as working with heavy horses or larger livestock
management. There were also reservations voiced by women too, such as a
lack of experience or confidence, and their lack of suitable clothing and
footwear, the purchase price of which was often prohibitive to them.
There was also prejudice, especially the way they would be regarded: the
Victorian attitude of a woman land worker being considered socially inferior
to a domestic servant was still very much in evidence (and would still linger
on in the Second World War).

When the war did not end at Christmas 1914 and began to spread to
new theatres around the world, concerns began to be raised over Britain's
reliance on high levels of imported foods. One prominent voice was that of
William Waldgrave Palmer, the second Earl of Selbourne, who had been
appointed President of the Board of Agriculture in May 1915. He raised the
issue of food supplies in a prolonged conflict, and a committee was raised,
chaired by Viscount Milner, which included Selbourne, Rowland Prothero
(later Lord Ernle, who would succeed Selbourne as the next President of

the Board of Agriculture) and the Right Honourable Francis Acland, to investigate how home food production could be organised. The committee's findings laid out sensible plans for an improvement of farming methods and an expansion of land under cultivation and recommended an investigation into food distribution. However, implementation was slow and frustrating, not least for Selbourne, who, seeing the danger of a war of attrition, pressed for and achieved sanction for the creation of County War Agricultural Committees (CWACs) during the autumn of 1915. Under this scheme County Councils were requested by the President of the Board of Agriculture and Fisheries to set up these committees to ascertain the needs of farmers and the best means of assisting them in cultivating their land, to train women for farm work, and to develop the agricultural resources within each county. Further District sub-committees were then established; their duties included the survey of uncultivated land, registration of all holdings over 5 acres, allocation of temporary labour, co-ordination of supply and distribution of manure, and cultivation of crops and vegetables. Sub-committees also monitored what happened to the land in their area and questions would be put formally to landowners who reduced their productive land by the construction of the likes of tennis courts or bowling greens on land that could have been used for growing food. It was Selbourne who encouraged these new committees to pay particular attention to the utilisation and organisation of women for farm work.

Two members of the Forage Corps proudly displaying their breeches, c.1916.

In 1914 a number of war-raised women's units such as the Women's Defence Relief Corps and the Women's Legion had created agricultural divisions and sent women for land work, but the numbers involved were low. One of the greatest contributions to furthering the employment of women on the land at this time was made by the Women's Farm and Garden Union (WFGU), established in 1899, which launched an experimental training course in farm work 'for educated women'. Local initiatives were also undertaken and good ground was made by the CWACs, which staged patriotic agricultural competitions that included classes for men and women, opening the eyes of many sceptical farmers to the abilities of women in farming. Some ground was already being made, and women were recruited to help meet the massive demand for horse fodder; the Women's Forage Corps was formed by a government initiative and administered by the Army Service Corps in 1915.

In early 1916 representatives of the WFGU met with the Board of Agriculture to discuss proactive recruitment, training and deployment of increased numbers of women in agriculture, and in February 1916 the Women's National Land Service Corps (WNLSC, later known simply as the Women's Land Corps) was formed as an offshoot of the WFGU under Mrs Louisa Wilkins. It employed new initiatives such as direct mailing of recruitment material to schools, hockey and lacrosse clubs, as well as staging public recruitment events, and one of its most important developments was the organisation of village women into working gangs under leaders. Some two thousand volunteers came forward as a result and by September 1916 it was announced that eight hundred women had been trained under the WFGU and 1,321 women had been found placements on farms.

The problem was that the situation of food production on the land at that time was not a good one. The spring of 1916 had been wet and snowy, affecting spring sowing, and hours of sunshine through the year were markedly reduced – hardly the best recipe for a good harvest to support a country in wartime. In late 1916 the President of the Board of Agriculture summed up the mood of the moment by going so far as saying, 'The victory or defeat in this great war may be brought about on the cornfields and potato lands of Great Britain.'

The cold winter of 1916–17 dragged on, with frost experienced in some areas up to April; as the year progressed, the cold, wet winters of the past two years and many instances of flooding began take their toll on the yields of British farms. In the opening months of 1917 the situation in the English Channel was desperate: Germany had lifted its restrictions on submarine warfare, and in February 1917 the German Navy sank 230 ships bringing food and other supplies to Britain. During the following month a record 507,001 tons of shipping were lost as a result of the U-boat campaign. Renewed fears of a war of attrition saw the Board of Agriculture set up the Food Production Department (FPD) as a direct response to this. The role of the FPD was to organise and distribute agricultural inputs, such as labour, feed, fertiliser and machinery, to increase output of crops. The FPD officials were endowed with a wide range of emergency powers to enforce proper cultivation to the degree they could cross private property, dispossess inefficient tenant farmers and order new land to be ploughed up. New, streamlined, seven-man Agricultural Food Executive Committees were established; these drove on the land work and reinforced the policies of the FPD.

One of thousands of cultivation notices published during the height of the German U-boat campaign and an ensuing war of attrition in 1917.

Women's Land Army recruitment poster, 1918. (IWM PST 5489)

WYMONDHAM

PARISH COUNCIL.

CULTIVATION OF COTTAGE GARDENS AND ALLOTMENTS.

Owners or Occupiers of Cottage Gardens or Allotments in the above Parish, who are unable to cultivate the same, are invited to apply to the Parish Council for advice and help, at the same time giving the reason for non-cultivation.

Persons requiring Plots of land for cultivation should also apply to the above Council.

Applications made under this notice should be sent to the Clerk to the Council at his office in Vicar Street, Wymondham, on or before Monday the 5th March next.

JOHN B. POMEROY,
WYMONDHAM,   Clerk to the Council.
21st February, 1917.

Back in the December of 1916 the WNLSC had estimated in their *Scheme for the Organization of Women's Service on the Land* that an estimated 40,000 full-time female workers were needed to keep Britain fed, a number the WNLSC could not possibly manage under their extant scheme. A meeting between Louisa Wilkins and Rowland Prothero was held and it was suggested serious consideration be given to the creation of a dedicated Women's Land Army of mobile workers.

In response to this the Board of Agriculture created a Women's Branch and appointed Miss Meriel Talbot as its first director. In March 1917 the Women's Branch became a division of the FPD, and administration of the growing Women's Institute movement was transferred to the Board of Agriculture, also becoming part of the Women's Branch of the FPD. It was in that same month that the publicity and recruiting drive for a Women's Land Army began.

The need was there, and the firm foundations had been laid: following the 'Shell Scandal', the 'Women's March through London' had been staged in July 1915, in which some 30,000 women marched through the capital under the banner of 'We Demand the Right to Serve'. The pressure was on, and as a direct result of the Shell Scandal, munitions work was expanded. More women than ever were 'doing their bit' for the war effort and a new national organisation entitled the 'Women's Land Army' was formed, followed soon after by a separate Women's Forestry Corps (WFS) in 1917, which would be extended to include women required

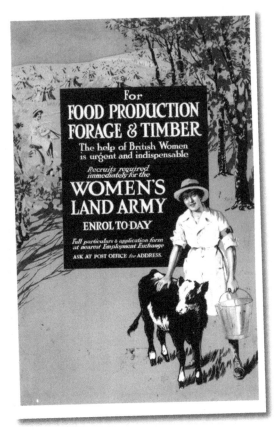

For
FOOD PRODUCTION
FORAGE & TIMBER
The help of British Women
is urgent and indispensable

Recruits required
immediately for the
WOMEN'S
LAND ARMY
ENROL TO-DAY
Full particulars & application form
at nearest Employment Exchange
ASK AT POST OFFICE for ADDRESS.

by the Timber Supply Department of the Board of Trade. At its height the WFS totalled two thousand members employed in timber measuring and general forest work.

The first Director of the Women's Land Army was Miss Meriel Talbot, joined later in the year by Lady Gertrude ('Trudie') Denman, who had agreed to take on the role of Honorary Assistant Director. The scepticism from the public in general about the ability of women 'taking the place of a man' on a farm was repeated, with further questions over billeting, a consideration of 'the loneliness of farm work', and wages. To address all these concerns the Board of Agriculture set up special sections dealing with training and hostels, county organisation, equipment and propaganda, and it was announced in March 1917 that training centres were being established across the country and that sufficient accommodation for women attending the courses had been arranged in large private houses or hostels near the farms where they would be trained. Wages were guaranteed to be at least 18 shillings a week (or the rate of the district, whichever was higher); this was raised early in 1918 to a basic rate of 20 shillings a week, and 22 shillings and upwards if they passed their proficiency tests.

Those wishing to join could volunteer at the rallies or apply for enrolment forms at a post office or employment exchange. Every applicant would have to supply three references obtained from the likes of their employer, their local minister and their doctor. Enrolment would also require the signing of a binding contract, initially 'for the duration of the war', later changed to options of either six months' or a year's service. Over two hundred special allocation committees were set up, before which candidates for the Land Army would appear. Here they would be given a medical examination and their aptitude would be assessed: those who could demonstrate some training would be despatched direct to farms, while those found 'strong and healthy but untrained' would be sent to a training centre. The Board of Agriculture was also keen to point out that girls under twenty years of age should be accepted in only 'very

A woman pupil at the Cheshire Agricultural College at Holmes Chapel being taught how to handle cattle during an animal husbandry course. (IWM HU 91978)

9

A 'Practical uniform for Women Working on the Land', 1917.

Members of the Women's Land Army on parade, c.1917.

exceptional cases'. Between 1917 and 1919 some 45,000 young women applied to serve in the Women's Land Army; of this number about 50 per cent were rejected. Miss Talbot, the Land Army Director, was convinced: 'We were confident nothing would be more damaging to the whole enterprise than the girl who would not or could not stick it.' About 23,000 were ultimately enrolled, who would then be placed at a farm for training. The period of training took four to six weeks depending on the stipulation of the local Board or the nature of the work in which the girl was to be employed.

Every successful recruit who signed on for a year would be issued

a 'uniform' free of charge, consisting of a soft hat, breeches, a knee-length overall tunic with a button-fastening integral belt, and high boots or boots (orders were stringent – two pairs of working boots were all a girl would be issued in a year); if she was issued short boots, buskins or puttees were also provided. A special measurement form designed by Mrs Spender-Clay, head of the outfit section, was given to each girl to fill in with her required sizes if she was unable to attend a store-room to be fitted. In many areas clogs and leggings were supplied from the summer of 1917, and mackintoshes and jerseys from the autumn. She would also be granted free bed and board in a depot for up to four weeks if out of employment (through no fault of her own) and free railway travel when taking up or changing her place of employment.

Women's Agriculture Committees were established in every county; County offices were opened and Organising Secretaries appointed, often with very keen and enthusiastic support from two or three Honorary Secretaries; then followed the appointment of the Travelling Inspectors, and of Group Leaders, who would receive slightly higher wages, the latter also being distinguished by an armlet emblazoned with the word 'Leader'.

Recruitment campaigns appeared in the press, the first appearing in mid-April 1917 when ten thousand 'strong, healthy women' were 'wanted at once' to become milkmaids on dairy farms in England, Scotland and Wales. Open-air recruitment rallies were also staged, along with more local appeals for recruits. Lady Denman herself delivered many of the early recruiting appeals in the southern counties where she, with her companion Nellie Grant, would dress in Land Army uniform and drive a car to a suitable high street or marketplace, announce their arrival with the ear-splitting noise of an old police rattle, and deliver rousing speeches using the car as an impromptu podium. In the first week of the Land Army recruitment campaign over 2,400 enrolment applications had been received; soon the number would reach five thousand and by September 1917, 247 training centres had been established and over two thousand women had been found farm placements. Despite initial scepticism the efficient organisation and training of the Land Army girls proved their worth to the farmers. Crucially, the weather also improved; food production was up and the wheat harvest of 1917 was hailed as the best in our history. Although this was a great achievement there was still a fear among many people that the country was running out of food; the Land Army was still deemed to be a very valuable asset to Britain's war effort.

LAND ARMY SONG

(Sung to the tune, *Come Lasses and Lads*)

The men must take the swords,
And we must take the ploughs,
Our front is where the wheat grows fair,
Our Colours, orchard boughs.
Our front is where the wheat grows fair,
Our Colours, orchard boughs.

In January 1918 the Women's Land Army was divided into three sections:

1. Agriculture
2. Timber cutting
3. Forage

Land girls working in agriculture would usually attend a training course, originally of four weeks' duration, extended by 1918 to six weeks with efficiency tests introduced to 'encourage the recruits to make every endeavour to become competent, and [give] the organising secretaries some idea of the skill of the candidate so that the woman could be suitably placed'. The majority of the training undergone by Land Girl recruits consisted of correct use of farm implements, care of young livestock and working with horses. Once placed, the majority of agricultural Land Girls were employed in the cultivation of potatoes, corn and horticultural produce. This could entail ploughing (previously an entirely male occupation), seeding the ground by broadcast sowing, hoeing or 'chopping out' the weeds and harvesting. They could also be charged with the feeding and care of livestock (such as chickens for egg production or cows for milking) and dairy work such as the manufacture of cheese – all the essentials to keep Britain fed.

A member of the Women's Land Army using a plough drawn by two underfed horses. Most horses had been requisitioned for the war effort. Those remaining for farm work were usually in poor condition, overworked and underfed. (IWM Q 30658)

Lambing was also considered suitable work for Land Girls.

Further proficiency skills taught to members of the WLA included mole trapping, farriery for agricultural purposes, and even training in thatching hay and flax stacks, which was introduced during the summer of 1918. Although treated with the same contempt and mistrust that the Land Girls had suffered, tractors were the new driving force on the land, and essential if production was to be maximised in Britain. Many of the first drivers of the 'new' tractors were, therefore, women and the first courses in motor tractor driving for women mechanics were created at the Harper Adams Agricultural College in Shropshire in September 1918.

Milking and dairying – ideal work for a Land Girl! (IWM Q 30681)

Women forestry workers loading logs on to a horse-drawn sledge for transportation in woodland at Cross in Hand, Heathfield, Sussex. (IWM Q 106565)

Timber cutting would require girls to have 'a good general education' and would entail most girls attending a four- to six-week training course to learn the craft. The skills they were taught included how to girth trees immediately after felling, finding their cubic content, and how to decide where to mark where they should be sawn. Advanced training for forewomen planters was provided at the Woodmen's School at Lydney, Gloucestershire. Once trained the placed girls would be employed sizing and felling trees, stacking and carting. They would then saw branches and trunks into lengths for such things as pit props for mines, trench poles, barbed-wire posts, railway sleepers and a host of other military requirements.

The WLA inherited the Forage Corps in 1917. Women in this section would often be working in a team or 'gang' of about eight, usually containing three soldiers, who would travel from farm to farm with a steam baling machine, baling hay or straw. Many also worked in chaffing depots, chopping

Members of the Forage Corps at the East Dereham Chaffing Store, 1917.

the hay or straw into short lengths for horse fodder at a forage store. Land Girls working within the Forage Section had to sign up for a minimum of one year's service. If she showed suitable ability a girl could be promoted to 'Corporal' in charge of her work gang; she would then act as a supervisor of labour and as an intermediary. Another promotion could be to 'Conductress'; this woman was responsible for the issue of food to her team and for the wire and oil required by the balers who accompanied the loads of hay from the farm to the railway or nearest chaffing depot. There are examples of a conductress wearing three military-style 'Sergeant's' stripes on her overall. Further promotion could come in the form of 'Forwarding Supervisor'; this role – usually carried out by a female officer – had the responsibility of receiving the cart loads of hay, organising their despatch and filing a report to the Department for accounting purposes. Many Forwarding Supervisors had large areas to regulate and can often be seen wearing hats with goggles and storm flaps, gauntlets and breeches under their skirts so they could ride a motorcycle. Many of the Forage Corps officers continued to wear their old uniforms until the end of the war, as did many women members, who continued also to wear their old hats bearing the brass letters 'FC'.

The importance of the work of the Land Army was appreciated but there were lingering concerns in some quarters about the girls losing their femininity, not only because of the hard-working nature of their labours but because the Land Girls wore breeches. Annie Edwards recalled the comments made by her local minister's wife when she went to obtain one of her references to join the Land Army: 'She admired me in every way of my life excepting she objected to me dressing like a man and it's going to spoil me.' The minister spoke up for her (he had known her from her time in the choir), saying, 'You can't go on that breeches will alter her, she is a good girl.' With words of caution that she hoped joining would not change her, the minister's wife wrote the reference. The concerns over breeches were recognised in the *Land Army Handbook*: 'You are doing a man's work and so you're dressed rather like a man, but remember, just because you wear a smock and breeches you should take care to behave like a British girl who expects

This Land Girl with her newly presented arm band (marking her first three months of proficient service) certainly took heed of the advice, 'You can have breeches – but do wear a coat over them.'

15

NATIONAL SERVICE
WOMEN'S LAND ARMY

APPLY FOR ENROLMENT FORMS AT YOUR NEAREST POST OFFICE OR
EMPLOYMENT EXCHANGE

Women's Land
Army recruitment
poster, 1917.
(IWM PST 413)

chivalry and respect from everyone she meets.' The spirit of change was certainly marked among the girls from the middle class; with their country needing them on the land, it was patriotic for these young ladies to get their hands dirty (literally) in previously unthinkable ways. As one lady pointed out in a letter published in her old girls' school magazine, 'You haven't got to ruin your hands, one good nailbrush, one cake of soap, a pair of nail scissors, and a pot of vaseline – I need not tell you how to use them – and the soldiers are sacrificing far more than their hands, aren't they?' She also commented, 'You can have breeches – but do wear a coat over them. Don't try to be a man if you are doing man's work.' The recruiting literature was always keen to point out that as a member of the Land Army people will 'admire your independence and your modesty, your frankness and enthusiasm; show them that an English girl who is working for her country on the land is the best sort of girl.'

And what girls they were. Margaret Huntington-Whiteley recalled her time as a Land Girl during the First World War:

I did it for three years and was never ill and never had a cold. I thought nothing of carrying a 100lb sack of bran on my shoulder up the granary steps and could tip up a cartload of roots single handed. At haymaking and harvest time a man did the pitching, while we girls 'trod' or stacked. At ordinary times we worked from 6.00am to 6.00pm with no half holidays and during the haymaking season we went on till 10.00pm and walked a mile or two home to sleep afterwards. I do not say we were not weary after the day's work but we were quite fresh the next morning.

There were concerns over discipline in the Land Army; many girls were in high spirits and saw this as one great adventure and a chance of freedom impossible in the years before the war. Letters of complaint and concern were published in local and national papers of girls failing to wear their overalls at all times (thus revealing their breeches) or girls going into public houses or staying out of their billets after 9.30 p.m. More 'effective control' was demanded, such as in the request from Lady Mather Jackson, Chairman of the Ladies' Committee of Monmouthshire War Agricultural Committee, to Land Army Director Miss Talbot, in which she complains: '[the girls] stay out late and do not often return to their farms until 12 and 1 in the morning … they are much talked about.' She continues, 'The Girls themselves, with few exceptions, do the least possible work they can.' She also complains of girls 'running away' from training centres. With the letter her ladyship included her suggestions for set timetables at training farms, including 'Bedtime – summer 9.30pm, Bedtime –winter 9.00pm' and a cutting relating to Grace Smith, who after being absent without leave from the Women's Army Forage Department was sentenced to fourteen days prison with hard labour. In her reply Miss Talbot was quick to point out that the Forage Section Regulations 'do not, in my opinion, lead to desirable results' and explained that such draconian measures do far more damage than good. With these sorts of comments in mind, however, and with a desire to ensure the girls were happy with their situations and were 'getting on', visiting

A lift on a cart is very welcome for these Women's Land Army girls. (IWM Q 30671)

Left: A Women's Land Army armlet dating from the First World War.

Centre: Women's Land Army, Land Army Agricultural Section proficiency badge.

Below: Presentation of an armlet to a WLA dairymaid at West Barsham, Norfolk, in 1917.

welfare officers were appointed. Mrs Cook, the Welfare Officer for Norfolk, soon reported, 'My visits are nearly all surprise ones and never once have I found a girl in any way slacking. On the contrary, they have always been hard at work, often cheerily singing over it.' The concerns over loneliness were also acted upon with the creation of *The Landswoman* magazine, launched in 1918; it was filled with announcements of forthcoming rallies, get-togethers, social clubs, photographs, as well as sections on cooking and gardening and competitions for poetry, essays, drawings and songs to entertain the lonely Land Girl.

To show some recognition for their efforts a series of WLA merit badges was created. After three months' proficient service (of no fewer than 240 hours) each girl would receive her official armlet, a green loden band with a bright red crown upon it. A round cloth badge to be worn on the left lapel or breast of the overall was awarded for passing efficiency tests in tasks such as milking, horse work, tractor driving, stacking corn, hoeing and manure spreading. After six months' satisfactory work and conduct in *and out* of working hours, a good service badge was awarded, to be worn on the left arm above the armlet. Red cloth chevrons were also awarded, each chevron representing six months' work (no fewer than 1,440 hours); two six-month chevrons would be exchanged for a single red diamond, and a red diamond with an outline green diamond in the centre would be issued in recognition of two years' work. A Distinguished Service Bar was also awarded for outstanding devotion to duty or courage. Some Land Girls can also be seen wearing Board of Agriculture 'Land Worker' brass badges on the front or on the pinned-up side brim of their hats.

Women's Land Army, Land Army Agricultural Section good service badge for six months' satisfactory work and conduct in and out of working hours.

A red cloth chevron would be presented to the Land Girl for every six months' work of no fewer than 1,440 hours.

Board of Agriculture Land Worker badge, often worn by members of the WLA on their hats.

A fine study of a member of the Women's Land Army wearing her proficiency badge and arm band, 1918.

LAND OUTFITS, OVERALLS, BLOUSES, Etc.

THE "STANDARD" OUTFIT.

HAT. Stitched brim, lined, close fitting, shady. 3/11

COMPLETE OUTFIT 35/-

SHIRT. Well made and well cut. Buttons at wrist. 6/11

BREECHES. Tailor effect, laced-up knees, buttons at hips, straps and buckles at waist. Can be worn with or without Coat. 10/11

PUTTEES. Standard size. Army pattern. Full length, cut on bias, long tapes to fasten. 2/11

Sizes: SMALL, MEDIUM, LARGE

THE "COAT SMOCK" is a very smart Farm Overall with a tailor-made effect. It can be worn with the Standard Outfit. In Amazon 11/9, Mercerised Casement 12/11, Plain Zephyr 13/11, Khaki Jean 13/11, Munition Brown Jean 14/11.

THE "YOKE SMOCK" is a well-designed Farm Smock, smart in appearance, and can be worn with the Standard Outfit. In Amazon 11/9, Mercerised Casement 12/11, Plain Zephyr 13/11, Khaki Jean 13/11, Munition Brown Jean 14/11.

THE "IDEAL" HAT.

For Landworkers and others. Very smart in appearance. Brim is made to turn down to form a Storm proof hat as shown. Close fitting, light, cloth appearance, neutral colour, absolutely waterproof, and no leakage is possible. 4/11

With small Brim 3/11

All our Garments guaranteed well made and wearing parts specially strengthened

Agents:
Mr. FREDERICK PLUCK,
Complete Outfitter,
BRAINTREE, ESSEX.

Messrs. S. & H. BANBURY,
HIGH ST., DORKING.

THE "AGRICOLA" OUTFIT, as illustrated, is an ideal land-worker's outfit, well and smartly made. All wearing parts are specially strengthened and always give satisfaction. Price, in Superior Quality Khaki Jean, Overall (40 in. long) and Breeches (small, medium or large) 18/11. Puttees, per pair, 2/11. Hat (Khaki Jean or Waterproof), 3/11.

THE "STANDARD" Outfit is well designed and made. It is buckled at the waist and fits closely, thus permitting work to be done in ease and comfort. The "Agricola" Overall, the Coat Smock and the Yoke Smock can be worn with this outfit. The Hat, which can be obtained in Khaki Jean or Waterproof Cloth, is smart, comfortable and shady. Coat ("Agricola," Coat Smock or Yoke Smock), 13/11, Breeches 10/11, Puttees 2/6, Shirt 6/11, Hat 3/11.
COMPLETE OUTFIT 35/-

Please mention THE LANDSWOMAN *when writing to Advertisers.*

The Women's Land Army of the Great War was disbanded in 1919. Dame Meriel Talbot DBE wrote, 'The returns [taken in 1918 of 12,637 Land Army members] showed that the work was distributed as follows: 5,734 milkers, 293 tractor drivers, 3,791 field workers, 635 carters, 260 ploughmen, 84 thatchers, 21 shepherds.' Lord Ernle, Minister of Agriculture, wrote, 'The branches which have been enumerated [by the Land Army] have covered a wide field. In all of them women have excelled …. In driving motor tractors they have done at least as well as men. Here also light hands tell. As drivers they have shown themselves not only skilful and enduring, but economical.' From the day of the Armistice on 11 November 1918 the numbers of the WLA rapidly depleted and in October 1919 Meriel Talbot circulated a letter to the remaining members explaining that the WLA would be formally disbanded on 30 November. The Farewell Rally was held at Drapers' Hall in London on 27 November 1919, during which fifty-five members were each presented with a Distinguished Service Bar.

After the war many WLA members were happy to return home to become wives and mothers while those tempted to pursue careers on the land were guided away from practical 'hands on' agricultural work. As *The Times* put it in 1918:

> The future for women in agriculture lay in three main directions – as agricultural teachers and scientific research workers; in posts where trained intelligence rather than physical strength was required, such as bailiffs, forewomen, land agents and farm and estate accountants; and as joint owners of co-operative farms and market gardens, both at home and in the Dominions.

A number of Land Girls did take advantage of the free passage to the Dominions offered to ex-service men and women. It is also not surprising that, with the positive attitude of practical contribution to country and home, many members of the Women's Land Army and food economy workers went on to become the backbone of the many new branches of Women's Institutes that were being formed across Great Britain. The value of the Land Army in the Great War was proved beyond doubt and would be proved again in the Second World War.

Opposite: An advertisement for private purchase clothing suitable for members of the WLA; *The Landswoman*, 1918.

Certificate of appreciation awarded to Marginia Money for services rendered in the Land Army during the First World War.

Marginia Money

Every woman who helps in agriculture during the war is as truly serving her country as the man who is fighting in the trenches or on the sea.

Walter Runciman
President of the Board of Trade

Selborne
President of the Board of Agriculture

For a healthy, happy job

Join the
WOMEN'S
LAND
ARMY

CLIVE UPTON

For details:
APPLY TO NEAREST W.L.A. COUNTY OFFICE OR TO W.L.A. HEADQUARTERS 6 CHESHAM PLACE LONDON S.W.1
STREET

Issued by the Ministry of Agriculture and the Ministry of Labour and National Service

PRINTED FOR H.M. STATIONERY OFFICE BY W. R. ROYLE & SON LTD.—51-296

A SECOND CROP

WHEN THE WINDS OF WAR blew again in the late 1930s the valuable part played by the Women's Land Army in the First World War was not forgotten. Plans for the establishment of a Women's Land Army (WLA) to fill the gap left by farm workers called up to military service were laid early in 1938, when the organisation began a register of volunteers. It was always clear that the WLA would be headed, managed, administered and staffed entirely by women and just like its First World War predecessor would primarily be a mobile force consisting of women who were ready to undertake all kinds of farm work in any part of the country in the event of war. By June 1938, WLA county committees for local administration, recruitment, enlistment and placement had been established. In February 1939 Lady Gertrude Denman, a First World War stalwart of the WLA and leading light of the National Federation of Women's Institutes since 1917, accepted the post of Honorary Director of the WLA, and offered her home at Balcombe Place, near Haywards Heath in West Sussex, for its headquarters. Recruitment for the WLA began in January 1939, with a section appealing for volunteers in the *National Service* booklet of 1939, sent to every household in Great Britain. By early March over 4,700 applications for enrolment had been received, the Women's Land Army was officially formed on 1 June 1939 and women were already helping with the harvest in August before the outbreak of war on 3 September.

The title 'Women's Land Army' was always something of a misnomer because this was always a civilian organisation, operating under the auspices of the Ministry of Agriculture, and not subject to military discipline. However, some Land Girls did work in secure areas and came under military law. Some were bound by the provisions of the Official Secrets Act if they worked on sites such as those where camouflage experiments were carried out. When war broke out, some 17,000 volunteers had registered with the fifty-two county offices and over one thousand girls were dispatched immediately to placements on farms, and many more were on four- or five-week intensive training courses at agricultural institutes that had been taken over by the government.

Opposite:
Women's Land Army recruitment poster issued shortly after their move from Balcombe Place to Chesham Street, 1944.

Gertrude,
Lady Denman,
Honorary Director
of the Women's
Land Army.

A national minimum wage of 28 shillings for a 48-hour week was laid down for girls over eighteen (except where the local wages committee's rate was higher). Unlike in the First World War, conscription for men had begun in 1939 and with the call-up of the first age group (aged twenty to twenty-two) in October it was estimated that as many as ten thousand men would be taken from the agricultural workforce; the 25,000-strong WLA stood ready to fill their place. Some of the old prejudice against the ability of women to 'do the work of a man' still existed, and uptake of WLA labour in agriculture was initially slow.

WLA recruits had come from a wide variety of backgrounds but with the introduction of conscription for women under the National Service (No 2) Act in December 1941 the diversity of the membership became greater than ever. Under the Act the first priority was for women to join the auxiliary military services such as the Women's Royal Naval Service (the Wrens), Auxiliary Territorial Service (ATS) or Women's Auxiliary Air Force (WAAF); then came

Land Girls shearing
sheep in Hyde
Park, London,
15 May 1940.

the industrial priority to supply female labour to the shell-filling factories, followed by the small arms ammunition factories, and then agriculture including the Women's Land Army (WLA).

Women called up under the new Act would have a very similar process to earlier conscription procedures for men. A card would be sent out to the person being called up and she would be asked, with usually a week's notice if she was applying for the options of service in the auxiliary forces, Royal Ordnance Factories or Civil Defence Services, to present herself at the local allocation office (an address would be stated on the card) for medical examination, selection test and any further interview by a representative of the forces. If all was in order and there were no objections, she was in!

Women could also appeal against their call-up if they believed they could demonstrate hardship caused or had conscientious objections. When the Act was introduced, it was intended that there would be women members of any committee or tribunal hearing women's cases. About two thousand women chose to join the conscientious objectors register; around five hundred of them were prosecuted for a range of offences against the Act and more than two hundred of them were imprisoned. Many of those who were compelled to do some work chose to avoid non-military units or kept away from manufacturing immediately associated with warfare by joining medical services, women's organisations on the home front or the Women's Land Army.

A cheerful Land Girl cycles to work with her spade over one shoulder.

There were both city and country girls among the WLA recruits, and most were young – often in their late teens – and, although officially joining 'for patriotic reasons', most will admit today that they chose the WLA in preference to military call-up or work in a munitions factory. Above all, Land Girls wanted to 'get away from it all' – a good enough reason to escape from humdrum jobs and stifling homes. After sending off a written application, accompanied by two character references, girls would be invited to an interview to assess their suitability. They were questioned by a board of at least two members of their local

Women's Land
Army enrolment
form.

(E & W) 1.   **A**

WOMEN'S LAND ARMY

APPLICATION FOR ENROLMENT

*This application should be completed and sent to the Organising
Secretary, Women's Land Army County Committee*

SECTION I.—For Use by Applicant.

(1) Surname...
      (In Block Letters and stating whether Mrs. or Miss)

(2) Christian Names ....
....

(3) Age...
(4) Full home address ....
....

(5) Present occupation ....
(6) Usual occupation if unemployed or if different from
      that shown under (5).

....
(7) If employed, state Employer's name and address.
          (If own employer, state " on own account ")
....

(8) Employer's business...................................
Signature of applicant.....................................
          (Additional particulars may be entered here)

A volunteer
signs up with
a Women's Land
Army Recruitment
Officer.
(IWM D 8793)

Agricultural Committee. The minimum age for enlistment in the WLA was seventeen and a half, but it appears that girls of seventeen were often accepted, and even sixteen-year-olds if they looked as if they were strong enough to do the work. A medical examination was required, but in many cases this was a quick question-and-answer session with the doctor when he would ask about 'wheeziness', flat feet and varicose veins. The successful applicant would then be required to commit herself to the Land Army for the duration of the war by signing a pledge card upon which she would 'promise to abide by the conditions of training and employment of the Women's Land Army', which then entrusted 'its good name' into her hands. Girls could leave if they married, or transferred to other war work. The upper age limit seems to have been fifty, but many older women with relevant experience or social status occupied management positions in the organisation. In a number of counties, women considered too old to join the WLA formed their own Auxiliary Land Corps, often affectionately referred to as the 'Home Guard of the Land'.

Name ..... M E White .....

No. 876166 .....

You are now a member of the Women's Land Army. You are pledged to hold yourself available for service on the land for the period of the war. You have promised to abide by the conditions of training and employment of the Women's Land Army; its good name is in your hands. You have made the home fields your battlefield. Your country relies on your loyalty and welcomes your help.

Signed..... G. Denman. .....
Honorary Director

Signed..... Barbara Gra. .....
Chairman Committee

Date..... 16 – 7 – 42. .....

I realise the national importance of the work which I have undertaken and I will serve well and faithfully.

Signed..... M. E. White .....

Above: Women's Land Army pledge card.

Middle: A Norfolk Women's Auxiliary Land Corps arm band.

Far left: Norfolk Women's Auxiliary Land Corps membership card.

NATIONAL   **SERVICE**

As a member of the Norfolk Women's Auxiliary Land Corps, I hold myself in readiness to do part time work on the land when needed. ·

Signed..... A. Wakefield. .....

Village..... Hindolverstone .....

Signature of Parish Representative..... K. Reane. .....

"This card to be held by the member"

Left: Badge of the Women's Land Army 1939–50.

BE IN THE WINNING TEAM

JOIN THE WOMEN'S LAND ARMY

RECRUITING REOPENED

The Land Army has special need of volunteers
for milking and other responsible jobs

ALL IN A DAY'S WORK

IN THE EARLY YEARS of the Second World War, WLA girls would simply be found a place on a farm without any previous training. They were just sent to 'lend a hand on the land'. A uniform was issued, consisting of two short-sleeved Aertex shirts, one green ribbed V-neck pullover, one pair of brown corduroy breeches, two pairs of fawn-coloured knee-length socks, one pair of shoes, one bib and brace overall, one hat (described as a brown 'pork pie' type), one pair of rubber boots, a short mackintosh (never very well waterproofed), a belted 'duster coat' and an armband, normally worn only on parade (although they were often slipped on work clothing for publicity photographs). Later in the war, a smart three-quarter-length brown Melton overcoat, designed by the couturier Worth, was issued. A green necktie, with the letters WLA striped across it, was also issued, but had to be bought in some counties.

Uniforms were normally sent to the girl's home in a parcel, but some got a rapid placement and received their uniform only after they had arrived at a farm. Although it was far from flattering, the girls did what they could to make the best of their uniform for 'walking out' and parades. Some strung a bootlace through the hat to stop it blowing off in the wind, enabling them to wear it 'cowgirl' style, perched on the back of the head like a heroine in a Tom Mix film. Many girls found their bib and brace overalls too hot in the summer and cut the legs down to shorts. The 'city girls' (all those with no knowledge of working the countryside) certainly made a song and dance of getting into and walking around in gumboots. The sheer ineptitude of some city girls led to many funny tales and cartoons in local and national newspapers, but the farmers found their antics both frustrating and costly. They damaged tractors and machinery, while some even confused male and female livestock, with unfortunate results. Most of these girls were also shocked at the lack of toilet facilities in the fields.

Training the girls before placing them on farms was the only answer, and soon four- to six-week training programmes were established on 'model' farms and at agricultural colleges. Standard training consisted of milking by

Opposite:
Land Army
recruitment
poster, c.1944.

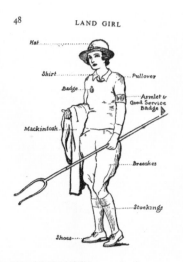

Left: *Land Girl: A Manual for Volunteers in the Women's Land Army* by Dr Wilfred Edward Shewell-Cooper, an organic gardener and pioneer of no-dig gardening (1941).

Above: The uniform of the Women's Land Army as illustrated in *Land Girl: A Manual for Volunteers in the Women's Land Army* (1941).

Right: One for the album – a Land Girl puts on her uniform for the first time.

Far right: Advertisement for landworkers' breeches from *The Farmer & Stock Breeder*, March 1941.

Top left:
The green loden
Women's Land
Army armlet
issued to each
member of the
WLA when she
started work
on the land.

Top right:
WLA armlet
showing three and
a half years' good
service (every 'half
diamond' equates
to six months'
service). Two
years is shown
by the red edging
and the two small
embroidered
'diamonds', with
the half diamonds
representing an
additional eighteen
months sewn on
to the armlet.

hand and machine, animal husbandry, tractor driving and hand work such as 'chopping out' with a hoe, followed by oral, practical and written examinations. Later, training establishments developed regimes that were tailored to regional requirements as well as running specialist courses in hedge laying, pest control and even thatching. However, if there was a great demand for help on the land, often at harvest time, girls would still be sent off without training.

Centre left:
WLA armlet
issued to county
staff after four
years' service.

Centre right:
WLA armlet in
scarlet presented
for four years'
service, with half
diamonds sewn
on representing
an additional
two years.

Land Girl
Rosalind Cox
(aged twenty-nine)
proudly shows her
four-year service
armband to local
farm labourer Sam
Scott at Bury in
West Sussex, 1944.
(IWM D 18063)

31

Right: Land Girls Eileen Barry, Audrey Prickett and Betty Long watch as Major M. Phillips demonstrates how to bait a rat trap as part of their pest control training on a Sussex farm, 1942. (IWM D 11227)

Centre: A wartime advertisement for rat poison.

Below: Members of the Women's Land Army begin to make hay as part of their training at the Northampton Institute of Agriculture, 1942. (IWM D 8806)

Anne Keys, aged twenty-four, drives a large tractor into a shed as part of her training at the Northampton Institute of Agriculture, 1942. (IWM D 8823)

Trainees harness a horse at the Women's Land Army Training Centre at Cannington, Somerset, 1940. (IWM D 122)

Once they had been placed at a farm for twelve months and had demonstrated good service and punctuality, Land Girls would be offered the chance to go on short residential courses relevant to their work or to take a correspondence course with an agricultural college. From 1943 a proficiency certificate and badge were created that would usually entail an oral or written test and a practical exam in the following branches of land work:

Women's Land Army proficiency badge in economy plastic, produced from 1943.

- Milking and dairy work
- General farm work
- Poultry
- Tractor driving
- Outside gardening and glasshouse work
- Pest destruction

An example of the examination content is exemplified by the Hand Milking examination. The practical element had marks for the following points:

- Personal cleanliness and suitability of dress
- Management and grooming of the cow
- Skill in milking (style, grip and motion)
- Efficient stripping
- Sediment test
- Time taken by candidate

The oral examination would consist of questions on:

- Feeding and herd management (calving, infectious diseases, etc.)
- Calf-rearing (including feeding and ailments)
- Dairy work (including milk-cooling, sterilising of utensils and reasons for producing clean milk)

At first, wages were paid by the farmers who employed Land Girls. However, the actions of a few tight-fisted individuals led to the establishment of a minimum weekly wage for girls over the age of eighteen of £1 2s 6d (after deductions for board and lodging). WLA pay always seemed (and in reality often was) just that little bit less than that given to men doing the same work. After 1942 the County War Agricultural Executive Committees took over the employment and payment of WLA girls. The girls were supposed to be employed on the same terms and conditions as other farm employees. A maximum working week of forty-eight hours in the winter and fifty in the summer was agreed, although most girls and farm labourers worked for far longer. Some girls were even expected to do their field work

Some of the seven hundred Land Army girls from all over Britain who protested for equal pay for equal work at Caxton Hall, London, in 1946. (IWM HU 63784)

Tin helmets being used for a novel purpose by Land Girls working on a Kent hop farm in 1944.

A charming study of two Land Girls (they are sisters) with their young charges.

Life in the Land Army by C. Falcon, one of the 'Better Little Book' series for children published by Tuck during the Second World War.

and help the farmer's wife around the house, carrying coal and cleaning grates. This was strictly against WLA rules, for Land Girls were 'outdoor workers'. It was also agreed that the girls should have guaranteed holidays and sick pay, most girls working for five and a half days a week, with Saturday afternoons and Sundays off. The farmer might even show his appreciation with an extra couple of shillings, or a few fresh eggs. All WLA girls stationed more than twenty miles from home were also granted a railway warrant for a visit home every six months.

The girls worked the same day, from sun up to sundown, as the men on the farm, but after a number of bad experiences in living conditions and in an effort to alleviate the old problem of loneliness for Land Girls, hostels for between ten and 120 girls (the average size was for 25–35 girls) were set up across the country in a huge array of requisitioned buildings as diverse as castles, manor houses, rectories, hotels, sports pavilions, converted stables and Ministry of Works hutments. Each hostel had its own warden, cook and domestic or 'daily woman', and a 'handyman' on call, or even resident in isolated areas, to maintain electric pumps, generators, carry out routine maintenance and

THE FARMER'S IDEA OF THE LANDGIRL

THE LANDGIRL'S IDEA OF THE FARMER

Land Girls as seen by farmers, and farmers as seen by Land Girls: published in *Punch*, March 1940.

repairs and odd jobs such as tending the garden. Care was taken that there was adequate provision of bathrooms with hot running water and toilets, a communal dining room and a recreation room in most hostels. Most hostels were also equipped with a laundry and drying room. Girls would often have to share dormitories with single beds or double bunks. By 1944 there were 696 hostels, 475 of which were run by the WLA, 146 run by the Young Women's Christian Association and seventy-five run by War Agricultural Executive Committees.

Land girls in hostels would soon get used to getting up very early to be 'bussed in', often on the back of a lorry or in an open trailer behind a tractor. Their work varied, like all farm work through the year, from ploughing

Cover of *The Land Girl* magazine, September 1944.

A smartly turned out group of Land Girls and the officers of their hostel, c.1943.

Queen Marie of
Yugoslavia (centre)
inspecting a
contingent of the
Huntingdonshire
Women's Land
Army, c.1944.

Land Girls on
parade at Wisbech,
c.1944.

and sowing and planting to harvesting. The most popular tasks were haymaking, looking after chickens, milking, and working with livestock but, as ever, mucking out and the hard, dusty job of harvesting cereals were never popular. Many farms were not able to replace their worn-out machinery, and some even had to resort

to horse power and long-redundant reaper-binders and hand ploughs when petrol was short. Crops such as sugar beet and potatoes were lifted by hand.

At the end of the working day most girls wanted to get back to the hostel, clean up, have something to eat and rest, but weekends and certain evenings would have entertainments laid on, such as whist drives and evening classes in subjects such as 'make do and mend', first aid, health, child welfare, keep fit and current affairs. Weekends would occasionally see the hostels lay on parties and dances but the girls would often hope to get out from those all-too-familiar 'four walls' and away to a local dance, perhaps on a military base with servicemen, and – who knows – perhaps a little romance.

To All Land Girls
From an admirer of their work.

I saw a Land Girl working
Alone in an open field.
Her, hard, once elegant, hands
A stalwart hoe did wield.
Her back was bent as she slew the weeds
That spoiled the potatoes' growth;
She never wilted, she never paused,
She had taken her silent oath.
At last the day was nearly done,
The sun was sinking low;
She gathered up her jacket
Then slowly cleaned her hoe.
She passed the chair where I sat
(I am feeble in body and sight).
She smiled at me as she said
'Been hot to-day. Good-night.'
We hear the valiant deeds of our men in 'furrin parts',
Deeds which bring the tears to our eyes, a glow of pride to our heart –
But when the war is over and peace at last restored,
I shall always remember the Land Girl, who made her hoe her sword.

An anonymous poem written in tribute to the Land Girls during the Second World War.

Opposite:
Members of the
Essex Women's
Land Army
homeward bound
with a cart full of
hay, June 1941.

LUMBER JILLS – THE WOMEN'S TIMBER CORPS

WOMEN were working in the timber trade in Scotland as measurers from the early days of the Second World War and their employment was soon extended to include general woods work; this led to the establishment of a Women's Forestry Service in 1941.

The Women's Timber Corps (WTC) was inaugurated by the Ministry of Supply (Home Grown Timber Department – HGTD) as a separate arm of the WLA in April 1942, to provide girls to work in forestry and timber mills. Many new conscripts of the WLA became members of the new corps; their uniform consisted of the WLA uniform but they were distinguished from their farming sisters by a special green beret and plastic Women's Timber Corps badge. Their kit was also supplemented with a pair of leather leggings (also known as 'buskins'), leather gloves, sou'westers and belts. Members of the WTC were entitled to six days' paid leave (exclusive of public holidays) during each twelve months of service from the commencement of their employment.

In England and Wales nearly one thousand members of the WLA already working in the HGTD or timber trade provided the foundation members of the WTC, while in Scotland the nucleus was formed by mobile women already working in the woods and living in camps. Chief Officers were appointed for each country, and Welfare Officers, many of whom had been working in woods for the HGTD, were appointed to each of the Department's Divisions, and training centres were set up to introduce WTC work to brand-new recruits over a four-week course. In Scotland, where the main demand was for workers to fell and prepare wood for use in coal mines, training was concentrated on general forest work but opportunity was given to volunteers to learn sawmill work and haulage with tractors and horses. In England and Wales, where the forestry work was more varied, specialisation began during training, in the first week of which recruits would be introduced to the four main sections of WTC work. Girls would not be expected to learn all the 'tricks of the trade' in a four-week course but, as explained in *Meet the Members: A Record of the Timber Corps of the Women's Land Army* (1945),

Opposite:
Vera Howson,
a Land Girl at the
Women's Timber
Corps training
camp at Culford
Suffolk, 1943.
(IWM TR 913)

43

Above: Badge
of the Women's
Forestry Service,
1941.

Centre: Women's
Timber Corps
embroidered strip,
worn on the upper
arm of the issue
jumper.

Right: Members
of the Women's
Timber Corps
using a double
saw to fell a
tree in 1943.
(IWM D 14099)

Below: The badge
of the Women's
Timber Corps was
cast in brown
plastic.

'they at least obtained a nodding acquaintance with the work, a respect for tools and an understanding of the need of timber for the war'.

At the end of their course candidates would be formally enrolled into the Timber Corps and presented with their cap badge. Many of them were sent to work in forests and locations a long distance away from their homes and families.

There were five specialised areas of employment for girls in the WTC:

General forestry work: lopping, trimming, preparing ground, assisting with tree felling and clearing up after trees were felled.

Sawmill work: operating a variety of machinery. A job that required precision, concentration and skill, it was not for the faint-hearted.

Acquisition: visiting woods and forests to select suitable trees for wartime requirements, and, when necessary, negotiating with the owner and drawing up the necessary contracts.

Pole selection: entering the forest before the felling commences to identify and mark the trees most suitable for telegraph and ladder poles or trees for similar military purposes such as obstruction poles for road blocks.

Measuring: a measurer helps the work of the WTC girl charged with selection and acquisition, then follows up with measurement and management of the incoming and outgoing timber at the mill.

Members of the Women's Timber Corps stacking pit props in a clearing. (IWM D 14104)

The work of the measurer and her mate, as related first hand in a wartime edition of *Woman*, provides an insight into the stoical outlook of the women of the WTC in general:

Measuring involves the holding of a long tape along the length of the tree and encircling the centre girth with another tape. In muddy weather, whichever of us does the girthing is the unluckiest. If you ever try walking round a log which is coated with mud you will know what I mean; but if you go one step farther and try to place a tape round its middle, I advise you to wear your oldest clothes. My 'other half' shares my daily life and between us we cope with the office management of the mill and are responsible for the entire measuring of incoming and outgoing timber. We share a small wooden

A member of the Women's Timber Corps fastening heavy chains around tree trunks on a wagon. (IWM D 14116)

hut in which we struggle with division, subtraction and addition, brew weak tea and eat queer sandwiches. In the summer it is a grand life but in the winter it is no good leaving your sense of humour behind. Not a spectacular job, ours? Perhaps not, but we have fun and we know we are doing really essential work.

The accommodation for the girls of the WTC was often sadly lacking in comparison to their WLA counterparts; the 'Women's Timber Corps Notes for 1943' booklet published by the Ministry of Supply was not very helpful when it explained:

If you are not comfortable in your billet, remember that feeding hungry members of the Women's Timber Corps is a big problem in wartime. You may be able to improve matters by showing more consideration and tact … If you are in a hostel remember that conditions in war time are likely to be primitive. Owing to acute labour shortages in the factories, much of the equipment that you would like to see is either unobtainable or its arrival has been greatly delayed. We at headquarters will continue to do our best as we have done in the past to ensure your comfort, but ultimately it is for yourselves, working through your committees, to see that life in your hostel runs smoothly and cheerfully.

Those working at a variety of locations also had unfortunate experiences in working conditions and accommodation, as explained by an unnamed Scottish WTC worker in The Women's Land Army by Vita Sackville-West (1944):

No matter what our destination, the weather was rarely kind; a state which did not lend a brighter aspect to the ever important question, 'Where are we going to stay?' The choice was probably between an expensive fishing hotel (which was in any case, on most occasions, too far from the work) or a 'but-and-ben', often lacking the bare necessities of life. We learnt to prefer the latter. There is nothing so disheartening as to come in from work, cold and wet, to find the bathroom and the fire monopolised by dear old ladies and gentlemen, in process of taking yet another rest in the country. At least the cottage wife provided what she was able so far as hot water and a bowl was concerned, and however large the family we always managed to squeeze in round the peat stacked hearth.

Recruitment was stopped for the WTC in July 1943 as other areas of employment for women such as munitions, factories and agriculture pressed a greater demand. In 1945 it was estimated that as many as six thousand 'Lumber Jills' of the WTC had served across Britain.

THE LAND GIRL

Anthea Shelmerdine

No. 5, Volume 7. AUGUST, 1946 Price 3d.

AVOIDABLE ACCIDENT

THE cyclist is undoubtedly the "little man" of the traffic world. In the welter of vast, roaring lorries, swift cars and flashing motor bicycles, he has much ado to prevent himself from being sent to the wall—both literally and figuratively.

His natural reaction is to fight vigorously for his rights and this is all to the good, although protests which have been made in the past by cyclists against a special cyclists' way on main roads seem curious to the detached observer. The speeds of mechanised vehicles, of cyclists and of pedestrians are differently determined and separate tracks are an obvious means of avoiding accidents. Observation of the large number of individualists who scorn the special way and pedal along in the main rush of traffic makes one sigh with exasperation at the obstinacy of the Englishman who prefers the risk of death to discipline.

A large proportion of fatal accidents happen to cyclists and there are a great many cyclists in the Women's Land Army. The other day a volunteer was killed when bicycling home from work—she was with two companions and they were riding three abreast in a narrow road. There have been other deaths due to going too fast downhill when there were dangerous bends or even a sharp turn at the bottom. Sometimes the victim, left alive to tell the tale, seems to think it an adequate excuse that her brakes were out of order. But whose fault was that? It is sheer stupidity to be carried away by a bicycle whose brakes you know are not working.

We all know the exhilaration of flying downhill on a bicycle and the pleasure of a nice gossip from saddle to saddle, but the occasions on which these innocent desires can be safely indulged in the English countryside are very, very rare.

It is often worth while to take a chance in life but never when the penalty of failure is death or injury to yourself or some other perfectly innocent fellow being. M.A.P.

HARVEST HOME

A T ITS PEAK IN 1943, the WLA counted 80,000 active members in its ranks. Although Land Girls did join in the stand-down and Victory parades, the WLA did not stop working in peacetime and was still actively recruiting in 1945. With the war over, however, many girls did return home; others left to marry or had their contracts terminated as men began to return to work.

In the closing months of the war, as government release and resettlement plans became known, Lady Denman became increasingly frustrated by their failure to include members of the WLA or WTC in any scheme of post-war benefits. In her letter of resignation, published in February 1945, Lady Denman stated:

> The Land Army is a uniformed service recruited on a national basis by a Government department, and the work which its members have undertaken, often at a considerable financial sacrifice as any branch of women's war work, is of great importance to this country. Yet they have been refused post-war benefits and privileges accorded to such other uniformed and nationally organised services as the WRNS, the ATS, the WAAF, the Civil Nursing Reserve, the Police Auxiliaries and the Civil Defence Services.

> This position is a serious one for Land Army members who will have as great need as those in other services of Government assistance in the problems of resettlement. As you know I have protested against the omission of the Land Army from various Government schemes and also against the decision, now announced, that capital grants to assist in restarting business enterprises will be available after the war to men and women who have served the whole time in the forces, the Merchant Navy, or Civil Defence Services but not to members of the Women's Land Army. It is this latest decision which has led me to feel that I must resign my present appointment and that I can no longer appear to be responsible for a policy with which I do not concur.

Opposite:
Cover of *The Land Girl* magazine, August 1946.

By this personal message I wish to express to you

MRS. M. KRENS

my appreciation of your loyal and devoted service as a member of the Women's Land Army from

18.11.1941   to   27.12.1945

Your unsparing efforts at a time when the victory of our cause depended on the utmost use of the resources of our land have earned for you the country's gratitude.

Elizabeth R

Lady Denman did not give up fighting for the rights of the WLA and sent a two-page circular to all MPs entitled *The Land Army's Case for Post-War Benefit*. The Executive Committee of the Liberal Party unanimously passed a resolution in support of Lady Denman, and the National Farmers Union expressed their support too, adding that the current situation was causing ill-feeling throughout the farming community. Queen Elizabeth (later the Queen Mother), as Patron of the Women's Land Army, also made her views on the treatment of Land Girls known. The situation was addressed to some degree only after nearly two hundred Members of Parliament signed their names in support of

motions and the Government agreed to resettlement grants of £150. Furthermore, a promise was made of £150,000 for the Land Army Benevolent Fund in England and Wales and £20,000 for Scotland. There was still not going to be any form of demob suit but members of the WLA were to be allowed to retain some items of their uniform on release.

Opposite top: The 'Personal Message of Thanks' service certificate bearing the facsimile signature of Queen Elizabeth, Patron of the Women's Land Army.

Left: Leaflet about the WLA Benevolent Fund, 1947.

THE WOMEN'S LAND ARMY BENEVOLENT FUND.

FUNDS RECEIVED BY MARCH 1st, 1947.

Raised by members and friends - - - over	£164,000
Grants by H.M. Treasury - - - - -	£160,000

The average number of grants made each month is 600.

LAND ARMY MEMBERS ARE HELPED WHEN NECESSARY IN THESE WAYS :—

Maintenance in sickness and when on compassionate leave.
Contribution towards maternity expenses.
Part payment of dental and optical bills.
Rehabilitation and training grants.
Free specialist's advice and assisted treatment for rheumatism.
Free independent legal advice in cases of accident.

THE FUND MAINTAINS :—

The Land Army Club where girls can stay in London.
Two Rest Break Houses by the sea.
35 beds at a country Convalescent Home.
A Homecraft Training Centre in Suffolk.

EX-MEMBERS OF THE LAND ARMY may also apply to the Fund for help in time of special hardship.

Applications should be sent through the Land Army office of the county in which the member or ex-member works or lives.

Opposite: Members of the Women's Land Army from across Norfolk after a Thanksgiving Service at Norwich Cathedral in 1945.

51

Right: Women's
Land Army armlet
presented for
six years' service.

Centre: Women's
Land Army armlet
presented for
eight years'
service, awarded
to Miss Marjorie
Evelyn White.

Below:
The Women's
Land Army badge
presented for ten
years' service,
authorised
in 1949.

Opposite bottom:
Women's Land Army
and Timber Corps
commemorative
badge awarded
to all surviving
members from
December 2007.

The Women's Timber Corps was disbanded on 31 August 1946 but 26,000 members of the WLA carried on through the darkest days of post-war austerity and rationing. In November 1949 it was announced by Mr T. Williams, the Minister of Agriculture, that, in light of the steady improvement of the supply of regular workers in agriculture since the war, 'the Government have been obliged to consider whether the purpose for which the WLA was established has been achieved and whether the time has not come to set a term to the existence of the organization'. At the time of the announcement recruitment for work with the county agricultural executive committees had been stopped; the last Land Girls were placed with individual farmers on 31 March 1950.

The final formal stand-down parade of the WLA took place on Saturday 21 October 1950, when five hundred of the remaining 6,800 members marched to the courtyard of Buckingham Palace, where they were inspected by Queen Elizabeth. *The Times* reported:

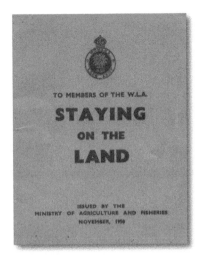

Her Majesty presented long-service badges and said that a farewell was always an occasion of some sadness, but their sadness could be lightened by their pride in their achievements. She had been their patron for the past nine years and their story had been one of great effort. They had observed the call of duty in the nation's hour of great peril and need, and the nation owed them an everlasting debt.

The Women's Land Army was finally disbanded on 30 November 1950. On release from the WLA every member received a release certificate that acknowledged 'with appreciation' the services given by the member named thereon and stated the exact dates that she had served as an enrolled member. A 'personal message' of appreciation was also sent to all members headed with the coat of arms and facsimile signature of Queen Elizabeth but, unlike their comrades in the Civil Defence Services and other home front organisations, the members of the WLA and WTC were not eligible for Defence Medals. It was over sixty years after the end of the Second World War, in December 2007, when the Department for Environment, Food and Rural Affairs (DEFRA) announced that the efforts of the surviving members of the Women's Land Army and the Women's Timber Corps would finally be formally recognised with the presentation of a specially designed commemorative badge. On receipt of her badge, Land Girl Hilda Gibson, aged 83, summed up the sentiments of many former members of the WLA: 'This recognition has taken a long time in coming. I think it will be appreciated by the girls who are left. It is something that shows for a little time you did serve your country, and to serve your country in its hour of need is a privilege.'

Above left:
Staying on the Land, a guide booklet for members wishing to remain in agriculture or horticulture after the final closure of the Women's Land Army in November 1950.

Above right:
Release certificate for one of the last serving members of the Women's Land Army.

FURTHER READING

Braybon, G., and Summerfield, P. *Out of the Cage: Women's Experiences in Two World Wars*. Pandora, 1987.

Briggs, A., and Beazley, M. *Go to It! Working for Victory on the Home Front 1939–1945*. Imperial War Museum, 2000.

Calder, A. *The People's War: Britain 1939–45*. Jonathan Cape, 1969.

Clarke, G. *The Women's Land Army: A Portrait*. Sansom & Company Ltd, 2008.

Collett Wadge, D. *Women in Uniform*. Sampson Low, Marston & Co Ltd., 1946.

Dakers, C. *The Countryside at War, 1914–18*. Constable, 1987.

Gangulee, Professor N. *The Battle of the Land: An Account of the Food Production Campaign in Wartime Britain*. Lindsay Drummond, revised edition 1944.

Grant, I., and Maddren, N. *The Countryside at War*. Jupiter Books, 1975.

Hall, A. *Land Girl: Her Story of Six Years in the Women's Land Army 1940–46*. Ex Libris Press, 1993.

Harris, C. *Women at War 1939–1945: The Home Front*. Sutton Publishing, 2000.

Huxley, G. *Lady Denman, DBE*. Chatto & Windus, 1961.

Jenkins, I. *The History of the Women's Institute Movement of England and Wales*. Oxford University Press, 1953.

Joseph, S. *If Their Mothers Only Knew: An Unofficial Account of Life in the Women's Land Army*. Faber & Faber, 1946.

Joyce, K. *Land Army Days: Cinderellas of the Soil*. Aurora Publishing, 1994.

HM Queen Elizabeth, Patron of the Women's Land Army talking with one of the Land Girls working on the Sandringham Estate, August 1942.

King, P. *Women Rule the Plot: The Story of the 100-Year Fight to Establish Women's Place in Farm and Garden.* Duckworth, 1999.

Kitchen, F. *The Farming Front.* Dent & Sons Ltd, 1943.

Mant, J. *All Muck, No Medals: Landgirls by Landgirls.* The Book Guild Ltd, 1994.

Members of the Women's Land Army. *Poems of the Land Army.* The Land Girl, 1944.

Members of the Women's Timber Corps. *Meet the Members: A Record of the Timber Corps of the Women's Land Army.* Bennett Brothers Ltd., 1945.

Powell, B., and Westcott, N. *The Women's Land Army 1939–1950.* Sutton Publishing, 1997.

Priestley, J. B., *British Women Go to War.* Collins, 1943.

Sackville-West, V. *The Women's Land Army.* Michael Joseph, 1944.

Shewell-Cooper, W. E. *Land Girl: A Manual for Volunteers in the Women's Land Army.* The English Universities Ltd, 1941.

Snelling, J. *A Land Girl's War.* Old Pond Publishing, 2004.

Storey, N. R., and Housego, M. *Women in the First World War.* Shire, 2010.

Storey, N. R., and Housego, M. *Women in the Second World War.* Shire, 2011.

Tillett, I. *The Cinderella Army: The Women's Land Army in Norfolk.* Tillett, 1988.

Twinch, C. *Women on the Land.* The Lutterworth Press, 1990.

Tyrer, N. *They Fought in the Fields. The Women's Land Army: The Story of a Forgotten Victory.* Sinclair Stevenson, 1996.

Ward, S. *War in the Countryside 1939–45.* Cameron Books with David & Charles, 1988.

Wilding, F. *Land Girl at Large: A Wartime Chronicle.* Paul Elek, 1972.

Wolseley, Viscountess. *Women and the Land.* Chatto & Windus, 1916.

INDEX